This Notebook Belongs To

_____

Enjoying this Notebook?

Please leave a review because we would love to hear your feedback, opinions and advice to create better products and services for you! Also, we want to know how you creatively use your notebooks and journals.

Thank you for your support.
You are greatly appreciated!

YellowBearPublishing

24983753R00069

Made in the USA
San Bernardino, CA
08 February 2019